¡Cocino con Mamá!™

I'm cooking with Mom!

Ernesto G. Pino

Illustrated by Lisa Lee

Book Publishers Network
P. O. Box 2256
Bothell, WA 98041
425-483-3040
www.bookpublishersnetwork.com

Copyright © 2014 Ernesto G. Pino
Illustrations by Lisa Lee

10 9 8 7 6 5 4 3 2 1

ISBN 978-1-940598-10-9

LCCN Applied for in October 2013,
not yet received due to
government shutdown.

DEDICATION

For my Mamá, María Concepción

Rivadeneyra de Pino.

And for Rich, who still brings out

the kid in me.

It's early in the morning,
and Mamá is still in bed.

There's cereal in the cupboard,
but I'd like to cook instead.

I know I that I am little,
and the stove is not a toy.

Still, I want to learn to cook
even though I'm just a boy.

So I make a little noise at first
and then more of a rumble.

Soon Mamá is on her feet with a trip
and then a stumble.

Mamá says, "Ricky, *m'ijo*, it is Sunday,
time to rest.

"You are active, you are loud,
and you're certainly full of zest."

6

"Sí, Mamá, yes, it's true.
I am up. It's time to eat!

"Please, Mamá, por favor,
let us both prepare a treat!"

¡Cocino con Mamá! Mom and I,
cooking together!

¡Cocino con Mamá! Pancakes, please,
light as a feather!

Soon, we're both in our warm kitchen,
and *Mamá* looks in the fridge:

leche — milk; *huevos* — eggs; some *vainilla*,
just a smidge.

¡Cocino con Mamá! What else do we need?
¡Cocino con Mamá! We have stomachs to feed!

Flour, of course, that's *harina*;
and some honey — *miel pura*;

plus salt and baking powder —
that's *sal y levadura.*

9

orange

naranjas

10

Mamá puts on her apron,
and she ties one on me, too.

She gathers more ingredients;
there are many things to do.

She pulls out bowls – *tazones*,
and a pan – *sartén*. What next?

Mamá's rinsing off some...
oranges – *¿naranjas?* I'm perplexed.

11

"Instead of maple syrup,
we will make our own sweet topping.

"Now beat two eggs – *dos huevos*,
never stopping, never stopping."

In my hand, she puts a whisk –
un batidor, to beat.

At first I spill some egg,
so I'll try harder to be neat.

un batidor

whisk

13

I'm now a cook—no, I'm a chef!
Well, perhaps a chef's assistant.

Even so, I'll do the job
because I am persistent.

¡Cocino con Mamá!
This is so much fun!

¡Cocino con Mamá!
There is work to be done.

Mamá mixes the white powders –
sal, levadura y harina,

which she passes through a fine, fine mesh.
Sí, es muy, muy fina.

"This mesh," Mamá says,
"is a sieve – *un colador*, my Ricky."

"*Un colador, un colador,*"
I say. This word is tricky.

sieve   colador

17

18

The powders, all together,
are a beautiful white pile.

"I will place this in your mixing bowl,"
Mamá says with a smile.

And as she does, the eggs and powders
magically combine.

Again, I mix and beat and mix.
Look, a batter! Very fine!

¡Cocino con Mamá!

I knew that I could do it.

¡Cocino con Mamá!
See, there's nothing to it!

Pouring milk into my batter,
Mamá says, "You're doing well!"

Mamá's pleased with this young chef,
I certainly can tell.

She smiles and adds more goodness
into the bowl I'm beating.

I'm happy to be helping out,
but when can we start eating?

21

Mamá fills another bowl with *naranjas* and their juices.

honey

miel

She adds some *miel* to sweeten it.
Wow, what a topping this is!

A squeeze of lime, that's *lima*,
and *canela's* spicy bite.

Such a delicious syrup.
What a cinnamony delight!

"Please mix this well, my little cook,"
Mamá says with such pride.

And so I do. I'm proud as well.
That's something I can't hide.

"Your job is done," Mamá says
as she's picking up the mix.

"Now, time to make *panqueques*,
which is something I will fix."

"The stove is hot," Mamá says
as she seats me at the table.

"When you grow up, you'll cook them;
when you're older, you'll be able."

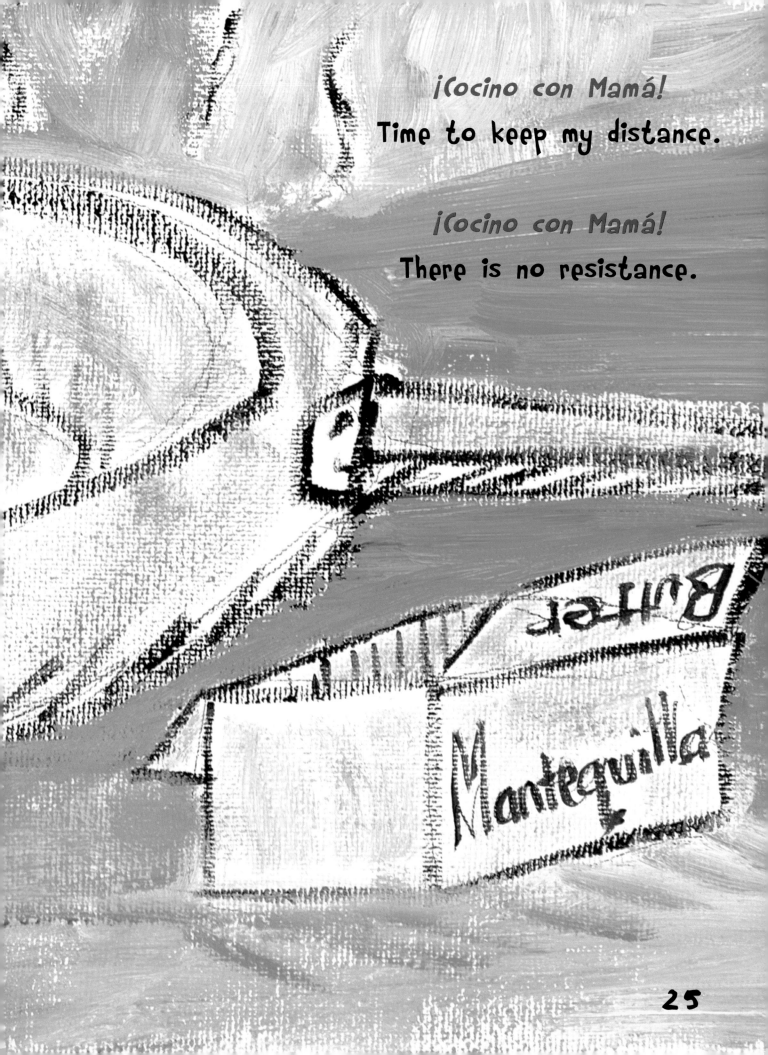

I watch as *Mamá* heats the pan
and adds a pat of butter,

which melts and coats the surface
with a hissing and a sputter.

Next, she measures out some batter
and she pours it in the pan.

I love to watch *Mamá* cook;
I think I'm her greatest fan.

And right before my eyes appears
a perfect, golden cake.

It's a very special breakfast,
which I helped *Mamá* to make!

Mamá serves me another,
and I gobble every bit.

When she offers me a third,
my eyes say *sí*, but I must quit.

I'm slowing down; my tummy's full;
my belt's about to snap.

Perhaps, just for a moment,
I might need a little nap.

¡Cocino con Mamá!
This food is a *fiesta*.

¡Cocino con Mamá!
It's time for a *siesta*.

28

29

30

Mamá lifts her sleeping chef,
and she takes him to his bed.

She tucks him in and strokes his curls,
then kisses his sweet head.

¡Cocino con m'ijo! My talented boy.
¡Cocino con m'ijo! What a blessed joy.

Fin (The End)

THE RECIPES

(Las Recetas)

PANCAKES

Serves 4

1 cup all-purpose flour

2 teaspoons sugar

¼ teaspoon salt

½ teaspoon baking powder

½ teaspoon baking soda

¼ teaspoon ground cinnamon

2 eggs, beaten

¼ teaspoon vanilla extract

1 cup milk

2 tablespoons butter, melted and slightly cooled

Grated zest of 2 oranges

Butter for cooking pancakes

Sift together the flour, sugar, salt, baking powder, baking soda, and cinnamon into a large bowl. In another bowl, whisk together the eggs, vanilla, milk, melted butter, and orange zest. Combine the wet and dry ingredients and whisk until just mixed.

Heat a griddle or large skillet over medium-high heat and add butter. Measure out pancake batter ¼ cup at a time and pour in batches onto griddle or skillet. Cook until edges brown and bubbles form at the top surface of pancakes, 2 to 3 minutes. Flip and continue cooking, 1 to 2 minutes longer. Re-butter the skillet and repeat for the next batch of pancakes.

Note: If batter becomes too thick, add more milk, 1 tablespoon at a time.

CITRUS-HONEY TOPPING

3 oranges, segmented, juice included

3 tablespoons honey

3 tablespoons water

2 cinnamon sticks

2 tablespoons lime juice

Place oranges and their juice, honey, water, cinnamon sticks, and lime juice in a small saucepan and simmer for 2 minutes. Refrigerate for 1 hour (may be prepared the night before). Remove cinnamon sticks and serve the topping over pancakes.

PANQUEQUES

Cuatro porciones

1 taza de harina

2 cucharaditas de azúcar

¼ cucharadita de sal

½ cucharadita de levadura en polvo

½ cucharadita de bicarbonato de sodio

¼ cucharadita de canela en polvo

2 huevos batidos

¼ cucharadita de extracto de vainilla

1 taza de leche

2 cucharadas de mantequilla derretida a temperatura ambiente

Ralladura de dos naranjas

Mantequilla para engrasar la sartén

En un tazón grande, cernir la harina con el azúcar, sal, la levadura en polvo, bicarbonato de sodio y la canela en polvo. En otro tazón, batir los huevos con el extracto de vainilla, la leche, la mantequilla derretida y la ralladura de naranja. Combinar los ingredientes en polvo con los ingredientes líquidos y batir hasta apenas mezclado.

Calentar una sartén grande a fuego moderado y engrasarla ligeramente con mantequilla. Verter ¾ taza de la masa por panqueque en la sartén. Cocinar hasta que la orilla esté dorada y se formen burbujas en la superficie, unos 2 ó 3 minutos. Dar vuelta el panqueque y cocinar 1 ó 2 minutos más. Engrasar de nuevo la sartén y repetir para el resto de los panqueques.

Nota: Si la masa llegara a espesarse demasiado, agregar más leche de una cucharada por vez.

JARABE AGRIDULCE

3 naranjas en gajos con su jugo

3 cucharadas de miel

3 cucharadas de agua

2 palitos de canela

2 cucharadas de jugo de lima

Combinar en una sartén los gajos de naranja con su jugo y la miel, el agua, los palitos de canela y el jugo de lima. Cocinar a fuego lento durante 2 minutos y refrigerar una hora (se puede preparar la noche anterior). Quitar los palitos de canela y servir sobre los panqueques.

English Glossary

Here is a collection of some English words in our story that may be new to you.
Next to the word is the meaning.

apron – An apron is something you wear to protect your clothes while you cook.

batter – When you mix wet and dry cooking ingredients, like the ones in our pancake recipe, you make a batter.

bowl – A bowl is like a large cup, and it can be used for mixing a pancake batter.

chef – A person who cooks is sometimes called a chef.

cupboard – In the kitchen, a cupboard is a built-in piece of furniture with shelves where you can store things, like cereal, plates, or items for cooking.

fridge – Fridge is the short word for refrigerator.

hissing – sn't this a great word? It's the sound the cold butter makes when it goes into the hot pan–HISS!

mesh – When you look at a mesh, you'll see that very thin metal wires are woven

together to leave tiny openings so that air or little pieces can pass through, like a window screen!

perplexed – When a person is perplexed he or she is confused or wondering what's going on. It's fun to pop your Ps when you say the word "perplexed."

persistent – When you are persistent, you don't give up. Ricky is working hard in the kitchen; he is persistent while he's learning to make pancakes.

resistance – In our story, when Ricky keeps his distance with no resistance, it means he stays safely away from the hot stove without putting up a fight because he knows that's the safe thing to do.

rumble – A rumble is a noisy sound, like thunder or fireworks on the Fourth of July!

sieve – A sieve is a fun and useful kitchen tool! It has a handle and a strong, round wire cup with lots of tiny openings. When you pour something through a sieve, it comes out the bottom smoother, lighter, or finer, depending on what you're putting through it.

sputter – Sputter is a fun word to say, and it means a sound, like lots of little pops.

stumble – A stumble happens when your foot gets caught or you trip while you're walking.

zest – Zest is a word that has two meanings in our story. We first see the word when Ricky's Mamá tell him that he has lots of "zest"– another word for "energy." Ricky has lots of zest! We also see the word "zest "in the pancake recipe. There, "zest" is the orange peel which is used as a flavoring. Yum!

Spanish Glossary

Here is a collection of some Spanish words in our story that may be new to you. Next to the word is its pronunciation and its English-language meaning.

batidor – (bah-tee-DORE) Whisk.
In our story, Ricky uses a whisk to mix the ingredients for pancakes.

canela – (can-EL-ah) Cinnamon.
Don't you love the spicy smell of cinnamon?

cocino – (coh-SEEN-oh) I cook.
This word is in the title of our story, *¡Cocino con Mamá!*, which means "I'm cooking with Mom!" Here's something interesting: In Spanish, when you write about something exciting, you start the sentence with an upside-down exclamation point!

colador – (coh-la-DORE) Sieve.
It's fun to play with a *colador*.

con – (cone) With.
The Spanish word, *con*, is in the title of our story, *¡Cocino con Mamá!*

dos – (dohs) Two.
Ricky and his mom beat two eggs for the pancake recipe.

fiesta – (fee-ES-tah) Party.
Who doesn't enjoy a fun *fiesta*?

fina – (FEE-nah) Fine.
This is another way of saying that something is thin, delicate or small.

harina – (ah-REE-nah) Flour.
In the Spanish word, "harina," the h is silent. Try saying it, *harina*.

huevos – (HWAY-vohs) Eggs.
It's not always easy to say a word that starts with the letters h and u. If you practice saying "huevos," you'll get it!

leche – (LEH-cheh) Milk.
Do you remember how much milk goes into the pancake recipe?

levadura (or) levadura en polvo – (leh-vah-DOO-rah en POHL-voh) Baking powder.
Just a little bit of baking powder makes the pancakes fluffy and light, and also helps them rise!

36

lima – (LEE-mah) Lime.
  Lime juice is tart and can make your mouth pucker.

mamá – (mah-MAH) Mother or mom.
  Can you count how many times the word "Mamá" appears in our story?

miel pura – (mee-EL POO-rah) Pure honey.
  So sweet and yummy!

m'ijo – (MEE-ho) Son.
  Ricky's mom lovingly calls her son "m'ijo." It's a combination of two Spanish words, "mi" (my) and "hijo" (son).

muy – (mooee) Very.
  Your mouth will make a funny shape when you say "muy."

panqueques – (pan-KEH-kehs) Pancakes.
  Another fun word to say out loud is panqueques.

por favor – (por fah-VORE) Please.
In Spanish and in English, it's nice to be polite and say "por favor" or "please."

sartén – (sar-TEN) Frying pan.
  In Spanish, some words have an accent mark. It looks like this ´ over the e in the word "sartén." The accent mark tells you where to stress the word. Try saying "sartén."

sí – (see) Yes.
  Such a fun and easy word. And, when you say it, it sounds just like the English letter C!

siesta – (see-ES-tah) Nap.
  In any language, who doesn't like a little snooze?

Tazón/Tazones – (tah-SO-nes)￢ Bowls.
  Tazones help make the job of mixing pancake batter so much easier and neat.

un – (oon) One or a.
  It's easy to say un.

vainilla – (vi-NEE-yah) Vanilla.
  These Spanish and the English words look a lot alike!

y – (ee) And.
  It's small, but it hooks up so many other words!

About the Author and Illustrator

ERNESTO PINO was born in New York City and is a first generation Latinoamericano, now living in Seattle, Washington. In *¡Cocino con Mamá!*, he happily applies his childhood memories of being underfoot in the kitchen with his *Mamá*, and as a cooking instructor he enjoys sharing his passion for food with adults and children.

LISA LEE is a creative artist and photographer. Originally from San Francisco, California, she now splits her time between Seattle, WA and the Bay area. She learned to draw and cook food as a young child and continues to share her talents with kids of all ages.